POP CLASSICS FOR TWO

Arrangements by Mark Phillips

ISBN 978-1-5400-6538-4

HAL•LEONARD®

Visit Hal Leonard Online at
www.halleonard.com

Contact us:
Hal Leonard
7777 West Bluemound Road
Milwaukee, WI 53213
Email: info@halleonard.com

In Europe, contact:
Hal Leonard Europe Limited
42 Wigmore Street
Marylebone, London, W1U 2RN
Email: info@halleonardeurope.com

In Australia, contact:
Hal Leonard Australia Pty. Ltd.
4 Lentara Court
Cheltenham, Victoria, 3192 Australia
Email: info@halleonard.com.au

AFRICA

VIOLINS

Words and Music by DAVID PAICH
and JEFF PORCARO

21
25
Play 3 times
29
To Coda
33
2nd time, D.S. al Coda
(take repeats)
CODA

ALONE

VIOLINS

Words and Music by BILLY STEINBERG
and TOM KELLY

Moderately

16
19
22
1.
25
2.
28

CAN'T SMILE WITHOUT YOU

VIOLINS

Words and Music by CHRIS ARNOLD, DAVID MARTIN and GEOFF MORROW

15
To Coda
18
3
20
3
22
D.S. al Coda
CODA

CENTERFOLD

VIOLINS

Words and Music by
SETH JUSTMAN

16
19
22
25
28
1.
2.

DANCING QUEEN

VIOLINS

Words and Music by BENNY ANDERSSON, BJÖRN ULVAEUS and STIG ANDERSON

19
22
25
1.
2.
28
32
36
D.S. al Coda
CODA

DUST IN THE WIND

VIOLINS

Words and Music by
KERRY LIVGREN

Moderately, in 2

21
1.
25
2.
29
33
D.S. al Coda
CODA
36
1.
40
2.

EVERY BREATH YOU TAKE

VIOLINS

Words and Music by
STING

12
15
18
21
24
D.S. al Coda
CODA

EYE OF THE TIGER

Theme from ROCKY III

VIOLINS

Words and Music by FRANK SULLIVAN
and JIM PETERIK

Moderately

12
1.
2., 3.
15
18
To Coda
3
3
3
3
21
D.S. al Coda
(no repeat)
CODA

I MELT WITH YOU

VIOLINS

Words and Music by RICHARD IAN BROWN,
MICHAEL FRANCIS CONROY, ROBERT JAMES GREY,
GARY FRANCES McDOWELL and STEPHEN JAMES WALKER

Moderately fast

16
19
22
25
28
31

I STILL HAVEN'T FOUND WHAT I'M LOOKING FOR

VIOLINS

Words and Music by
U2

Moderately

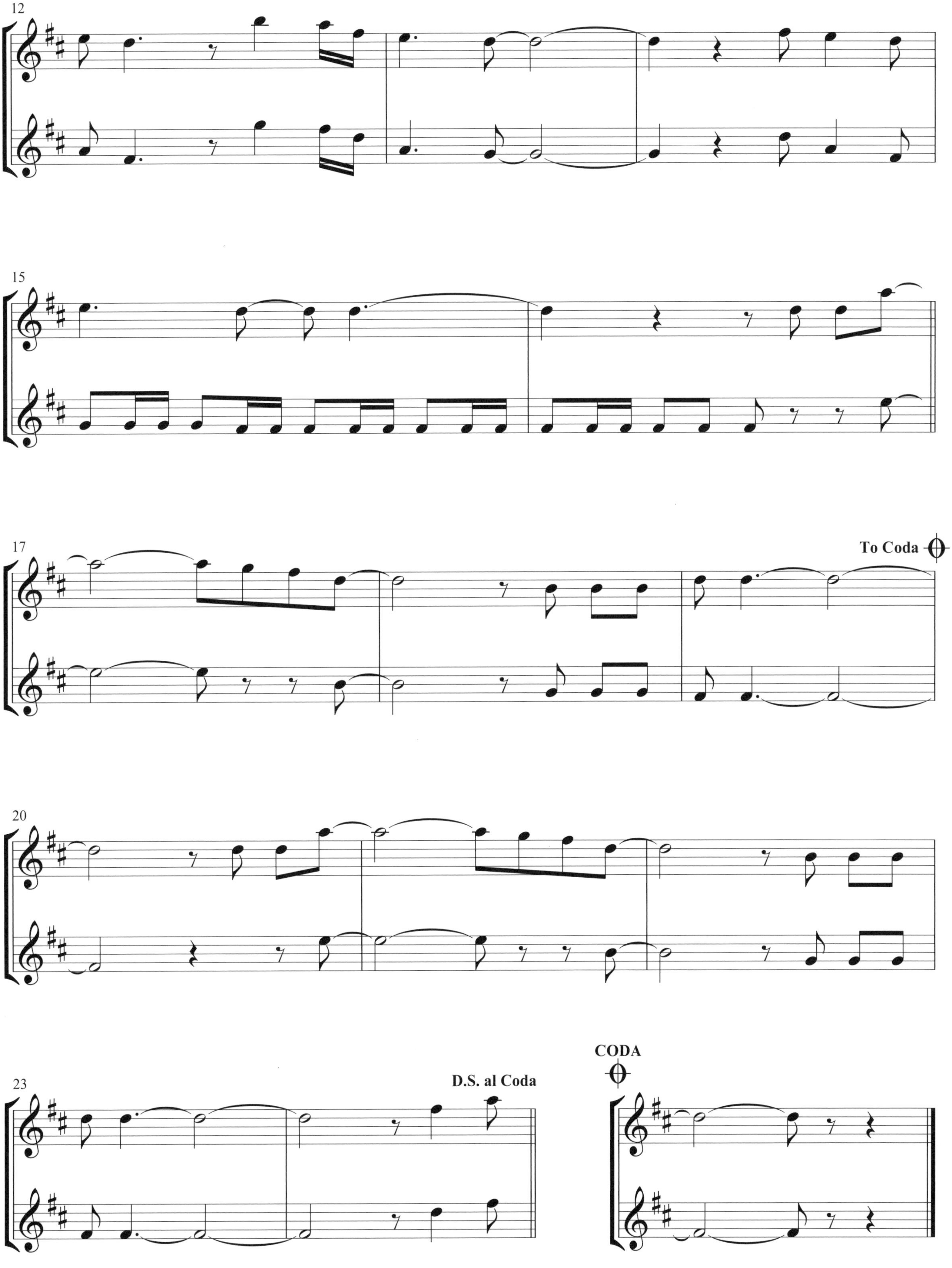
12
15
17
To Coda
20
23
D.S. al Coda
CODA

IMAGINE

VIOLINS

Words and Music by
JOHN LENNON

16
1.
2.
19
21
23
To Coda
25
D.S. al Coda
(take 2nd ending)
CODA

JESSIE'S GIRL

VIOLINS

Words and Music by
RICK SPRINGFIELD

Moderately fast

15
18
21
1.
24
27
2.
30

LEAN ON ME

VIOLINS

Words and Music by
BILL WITHERS

To Coda
1.
2.
D.S. al Coda
CODA

PIANO MAN

VIOLINS

Words and Music by
BILLY JOEL

25
30
35
40
44
49
To Coda
D.S. al Coda
(no repeat)
CODA

RIGHT HERE WAITING

VIOLINS

Words and Music by
RICHARD MARX

16
To Coda
19
1.
22
2.
25
28
31
D.S. al Coda
CODA

SILLY LOVE SONGS

VIOLINS

Words and Music by PAUL McCARTNEY
and LINDA McCARTNEY

(small notes optional)
1.–3.
4.
To Coda
D.S. al Coda
CODA

THE SOUND OF SILENCE

VIOLINS

Words and Music by
PAUL SIMON

15
18
21
24
28
31

STAND BY ME

VIOLINS

Words and Music by JERRY LEIBER,
MIKE STOLLER and BEN E. KING

16
19
22
To Coda
25
28
31
D.S. al Coda
CODA

SWEET CAROLINE

VIOLINS

Words and Music by
NEIL DIAMOND

22
27
31
35
39
43
2nd time, D.C. al Coda
CODA

TAKE ON ME

VIOLINS

Words by PAL WAAKTAAR
and MAGNE FURUHOLMNE
Words by PAL WAAKTAAR,
MAGNE FURUHOLMNE and MORTN HARKET

16
20
24
28
32
1.
2.

TIME AFTER TIME

VIOLINS

Words and Music by CYNDI LAUPER
and ROB HYMAN

19
22
25
28
32
To Coda
D.C. al Coda
(take 2nd ending)
CODA
35

WE BUILT THIS CITY

VIOLINS

Words and Music by BERNIE TAUPIN,
MARTIN PAGE, DENNIS LAMBERT
and PETER WOLF

21
25
28
32
36
39
1.
2.

YOU ARE SO BEAUTIFUL

VIOLINS

Words and Music by BILLY PRESTON
and BRUCE FISHER

21
To Coda
25
29
32
1.
35
2.
D.S. al Coda
CODA

HAL LEONARD PRESENTS

EASY INSTRUMENTAL DUETS

Start your duet playing experience with these fun songbooks! Over 20 easy duet arrangements for two instrumentalists are featured in each of these collections. Woodwind and brass editions can be played together as can the string editions. **Only $9.99 each!**

THE BEATLES FOR TWO

23 favorites from the Fab Four in easy duet arrangements for two instrumentalists are featured in this collection: All You Need Is Love • Eleanor Rigby • Here Comes the Sun • Hey Jude • I Want to Hold Your Hand • Penny Lane • Something • Yellow Submarine • Yesterday • and more.

00291024	FLUTE	00291028	TROMBONE
00291025	CLARINET	00291029	VIOLIN
00291026	ALTO SAX	00291030	CELLO
00291027	TRUMPET		

BROADWAY SONGS FOR TWO

22 showstoppers: Any Dream Will Do • Bring Him Home • Cabaret • Edelweiss • For Forever • Hello, Dolly! • I Believe • Memory • One • Popular • Seasons of Love • Seventy Six Trombones • Tomorrow • Where Is Love? • You've Got a Friend • and more.

00252493	FLUTE	00252497	TROMBONE
00252494	CLARINET	00252500	VIOLIN
00252495	ALTO SAX	00252501	CELLO
00252496	TRUMPET		

CHRISTMAS CAROLS FOR TWO

Songs include: Angels We Have Heard on High • Away in a Manger • Deck the Hall • Jingle Bells • Joy to the World • O Holy Night • Silent Night • We Wish You a Merry Christmas • and more.

00277964	FLUTE	00277968	TROMBONE
00277965	CLARINET	00277969	VIOLIN
00277966	ALTO SAX	00277970	CELLO
00277967	TRUMPET		

CHRISTMAS HITS FOR TWO

22 terrific holiday duets: All I Want for Christmas Is You • Baby, It's Cold Outside • The Christmas Song (Chestnuts Roasting on an Open Fire) • Do You Want to Build a Snowman? • Feliz Navidad • Have Yourself a Merry Little Christmas • It's Beginning to Look like Christmas • Let It Snow! Let It Snow! Let It Snow! • Mary, Did You Know? • Rockin' Around the Christmas Tree • Silver Bells • White Christmas • and more.

00172461	FLUTE	00172465	TROMBONE
00172462	CLARINET	00172466	VIOLIN
00172463	ALTO SAX	00172467	CELLO
00172464	TRUMPET		

CLASSIC ROCK FOR TWO

23 classic rock songs: Bang a Gong (Get It On) · Can't Fight This Feeling · Carry on Wayward Son · Cold As Ice · Come on Eileen · Come Together · Crocodile Rock · Down on the Corner · Every Little Thing She Does Is Magic · Free Fallin' · Hurts So Good · The Joker · Livin' on a Prayer · and more.

00303026	FLUTE	00303030	TROMBONE
00303027	CLARINET	00303031	VIOLIN
00303028	ALTO SAX	00303032	CELLO
00303029	TRUMPET		

CLASSICAL THEMES FOR TWO

24 favorite melodies from top classical composers: Air on the G String • Blue Danube Waltz • Canon in D • Eine Kleine Nachtmusik • Hallelujah Chorus • Jesu, Joy of Man's Desiring • Minuet in G Major • Ode to Joy • Pictures at an Exhibition • Sheep May Safely Graze • Trumpet Voluntary • William Tell Overture • and more.

00254439	FLUTE	00254443	TROMBONE
00254440	CLARINET	00254444	VIOLIN
00254441	ALTO SAX	00254445	CELLO
00254442	TRUMPET		

DISNEY SONGS FOR TWO

23 Disney favorites: Beauty and the Beast • Circle of Life • Evermore • Friend Like Me • How Far I'll Go • Let It Go • Mickey Mouse March • Supercalifragilisticexpialidocious • When You Wish upon a Star • A Whole New World • Zip-A-Dee-Doo-Dah • and more.

00284643	FLUTE	00284647	TROMBONE
00284644	CLARINET	00284648	VIOLIN
00284645	ALTO SAX	00284649	CELLO
00284646	TRUMPET		

HIT SONGS FOR TWO

22 mega hits: All About That Bass • All of Me • Brave • Can't Stop the Feeling • Grenade • Hey, Soul Sister • I Will Wait • Let Her Go • 100 Years • Royals • Shake It Off • Shape of You • Stay with Me • Viva La Vida • and more.

00252482	FLUTE	00252486	TROMBONE
00252483	CLARINET	00252487	VIOLIN
00252484	ALTO SAX	00252488	CELLO
00252485	TRUMPET		

MOVIE SONGS FOR TWO

23 blockbuster hits are featured in this collection: City of Stars • Footloose • Hallelujah • Moon River • The Pink Panther • Puttin' on the Ritz • Skyfall • That's Amore • and more.

00284651	FLUTE	00284655	TROMBONE
00284652	CLARINET	00284656	VIOLIN
00284653	ALTO SAX	00284657	CELLO
00284654	TRUMPET		

POP CLASSICS FOR TWO

23 classic pop hits: Africa · Alone · Can't Smile Without You · Centerfold · Dancing Queen · Dust in the Wind · Every Breath You Take · Eye of the Tiger · I Melt with You · I Still Haven't Found What I'm Looking For · Imagine · Jessie's Girl · and more.

00303019	FLUTE	00303023	TROMBONE
00303020	CLARINET	00303024	VIOLIN
00303021	ALTO SAX	00303025	CELLO
00303022	TRUMPET		

HAL•LEONARD®

Prices, contents and availability subject to change without notice. Sales restrictions to some countries apply. All prices listed in U.S. funds.

ORDER TODAY FROM YOUR FAVORITE MUSIC RETAILER AT **HALLEONARD.COM**